BRIGHT IDEA BOOKS

ZOOKEEPER

by Marne Ventura

CAPSTONE PRESS
a capstone imprint

Bright Idea Books are published by Capstone Press
1710 Roe Crest Drive, North Mankato, Minnesota 56003
www.mycapstone.com

Library of Congress Cataloging-in-Publication Data
Names: Ventura, Marne, author.
Title: Zookeeper / by Marne Ventura.
Description: North Mankato, Minnesota : Bright Idea Books, an imprint of
   Capstone Press, [2019] | Series: Jobs with animals | Audience: Age 9-12. |
   Audience: Grade 4 to 6. | Includes bibliographical references and index.
Identifiers: LCCN 2018035991 | ISBN 9781543557831 (hardcover : alk. paper) |
   ISBN 9781543558159 (ebook) | ISBN 9781543560459 (paperback)
Subjects: LCSH: Zoo keepers--Vocational guidance--Juvenile literature.
Classification: LCC QL50.5 .V46 2019 | DDC 590.73--dc23
LC record available at https://lccn.loc.gov/2018035991

Editorial Credits
Editor: Meg Gaertner
Designer: Becky Daum
Production Specialist: Dan Peluso

Photo Credits
iStockphoto: Image Source, 5, kali9, 18–19, Lingbeek, 26–27, Naked King, cover (background),
RollingEarth, 9, skynesher, 17; Shutterstock Images: a katz, 22–23, Anan Kaewkhammul, 14–15,
15, ChameleonsEye, 12–13, ellinnur bakarudin, 21, meunierd, 25, Milkovasa, 30–31, Tiffany Bryant,
cover (foreground), topimages, 10–11, wjarek, 6–7, Xseon, 11, 28

TABLE OF CONTENTS

CHAPTER 1

ZOOKEEPER

A school group goes to the zoo. The children look at the monkeys and snakes. A man brings a snake out of its home. He shows the snake to the children. He is a zookeeper.

Zookeepers work in zoos or wild animal parks. They take care of animals. They feed the animals. They make sure the animals are healthy. They keep the animals' homes clean. They find ways to help animals play. This gives the animals exercise.

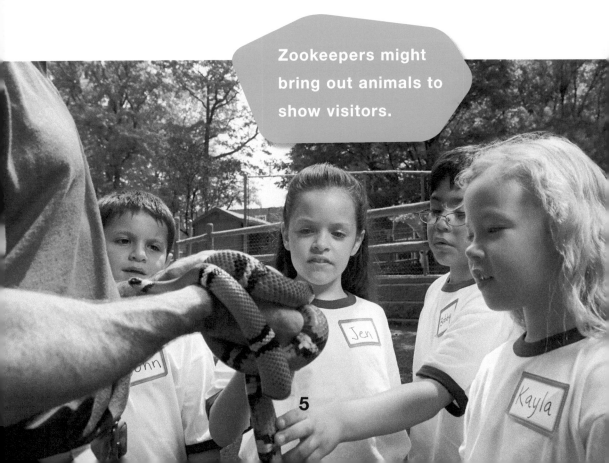

Zookeepers might bring out animals to show visitors.

Zookeepers work with people too. They call a **veterinarian** when an animal is sick. They may help scientists study animals. They talk to zoo visitors. They teach people about wild animals. They work to keep the animals and guests safe.

THE ZOO

The word "zoo" was first used in the late 1800s. It was a short name for the Zoological Gardens in London, England.

Zookeepers give talks about specific animals.

Do you love wild animals? Would you like to work with them? Maybe a job as a zookeeper is for you.

CHAPTER 2

QUALITIES AND
Skills

Good zookeepers love all kinds of animals. But they focus on certain **species**. Some care for big cats such as lions. Others care for birds. Others take care of snakes.

Zookeepers are creative. Wild animals run free. Zoo animals live in smaller spaces. Zookeepers find ways to keep them busy. They hide food for animals to find. They play games to give animals exercise.

Zookeepers can develop close bonds with animals.

A zookeeper greets an elephant before cleaning its home.

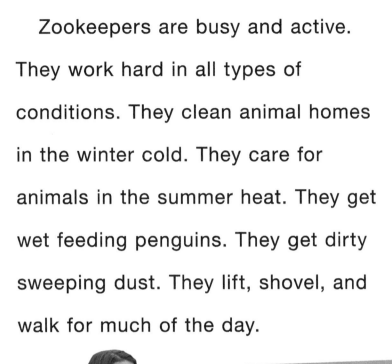

Zookeepers are busy and active. They work hard in all types of conditions. They clean animal homes in the winter cold. They care for animals in the summer heat. They get wet feeding penguins. They get dirty sweeping dust. They lift, shovel, and walk for much of the day.

Some zookeepers train animals for shows.

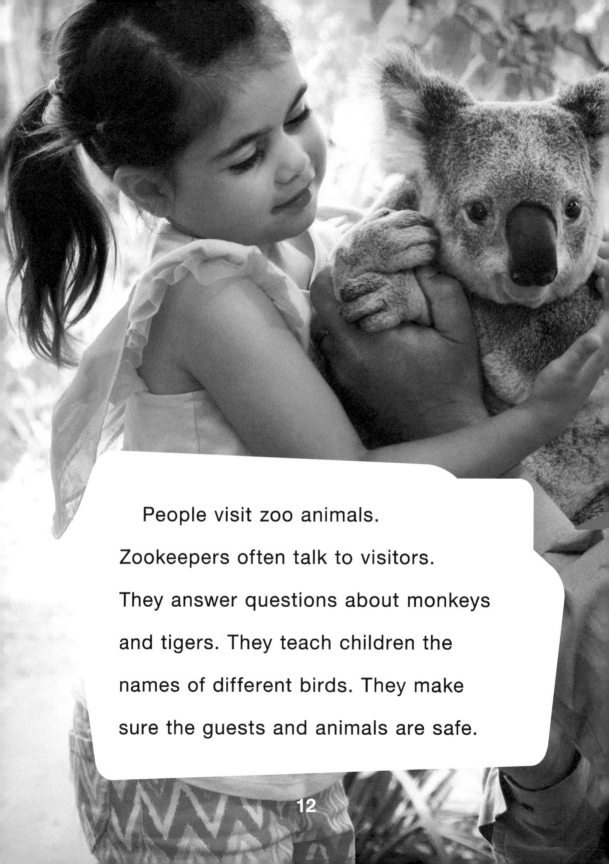

People visit zoo animals.
Zookeepers often talk to visitors.
They answer questions about monkeys
and tigers. They teach children the
names of different birds. They make
sure the guests and animals are safe.

Zookeepers help animals and people interact safely.

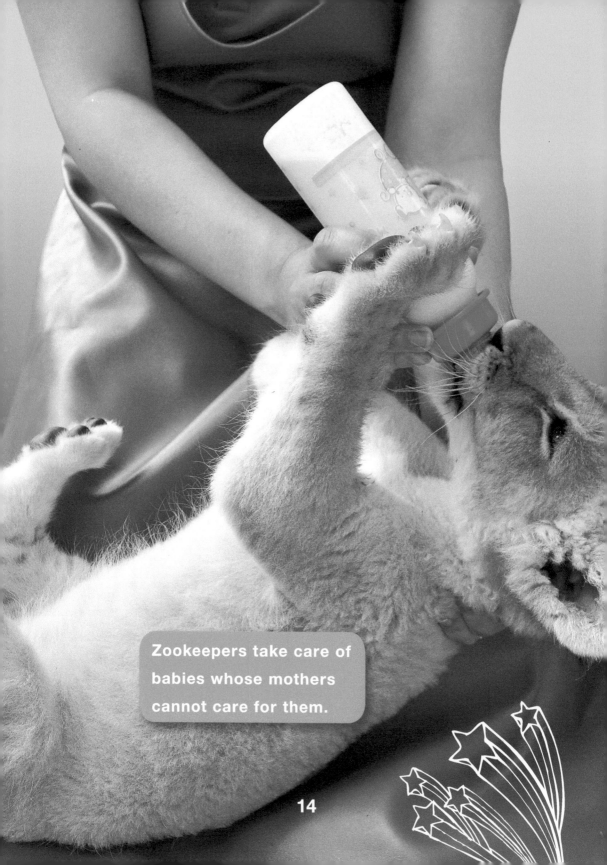

Zookeepers take care of babies whose mothers cannot care for them.

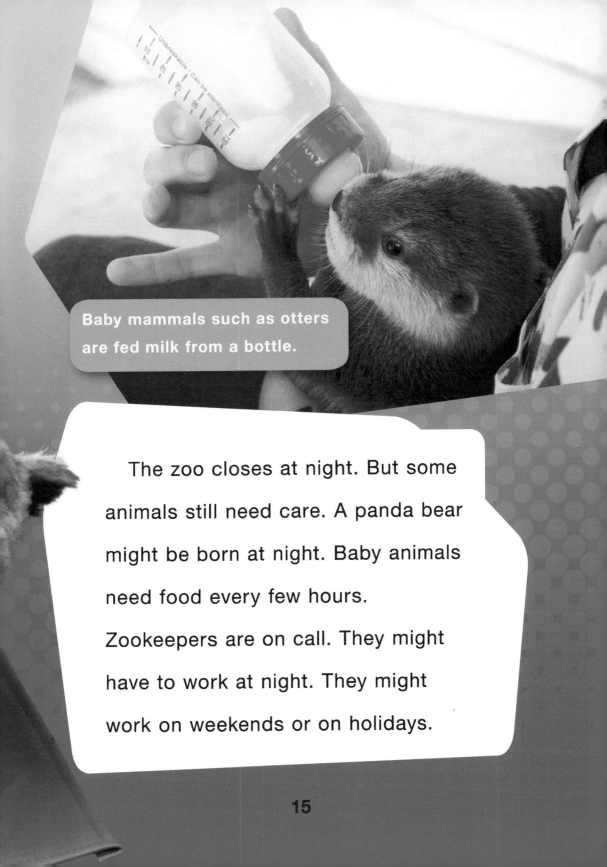

Baby mammals such as otters are fed milk from a bottle.

The zoo closes at night. But some animals still need care. A panda bear might be born at night. Baby animals need food every few hours. Zookeepers are on call. They might have to work at night. They might work on weekends or on holidays.

CHAPTER 3

SCHOOL FOR
Zookeepers

Zookeepers do not have to go to college. But job options are better for those who do. There are four-year and two-year **degrees** for zookeepers. Some colleges have programs in zookeeping. Others offer degrees in **animal science** and animal **behavior**.

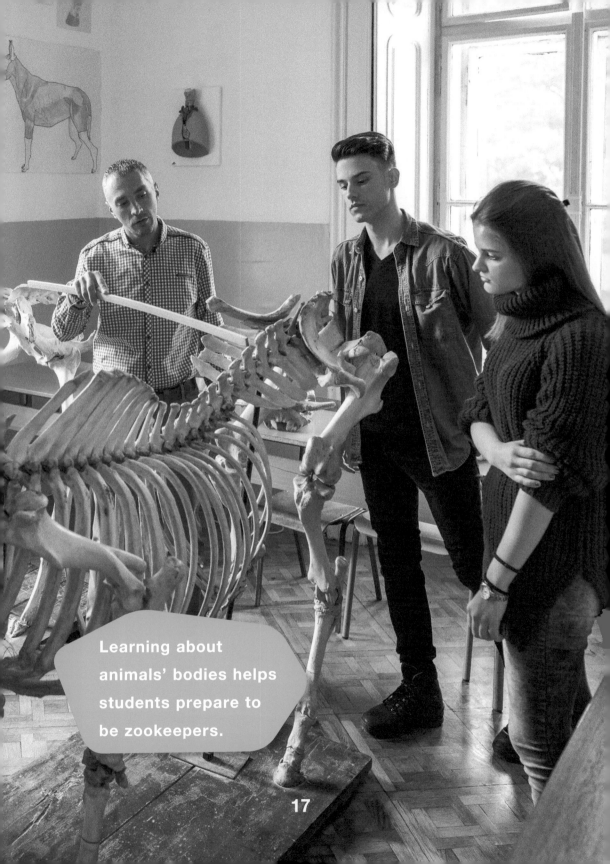

Learning about animals' bodies helps students prepare to be zookeepers.

Would you like to be a zookeeper? You can start learning now. Future zookeepers should learn math and **biology**. They should also do well in English. Public speaking skills are helpful. Read books and watch TV shows about wildlife. Visit animals at the zoo.

ZOO VETS

Zoo vets treat the animals in zoos. Vets give medicine to sick animals. They help animals that are hurt.

Visitors can learn a lot at zoo talks.

CHAPTER 4

GETTING
Experience

Going to school is one way to learn about animals. But people can also get experience with helping animals.

Some zoos take **volunteers**. Others

have summer programs for students.

You can also ask to help at wild animal

parks and **aquariums**.

Some volunteers talk to visitors or help feed the animals.

You can care for cats and dogs at shelters. This will help prepare you for their wilder relatives at zoos.

Many animal shelters and pet clinics take volunteers. Volunteers feed and clean up after the animals. They play with them. They help the animals get exercise. You can practice working with animals. Your experience may help you get a job later.

CHAPTER 5

JOBS

Many people apply for every zookeeper job. Not every city has a zoo or wild animal park. You might need to move to a different city. Sometimes people start out in a different zoo job. There are many other jobs at zoos. People wait until a zookeeper job opens up.

People might sell tickets at the zoo while they wait for a zookeeping job.

Tickets & Tours

The pay is not high for zookeepers. They earn around $25,000 per year on average. But they get to spend time in nature. They enjoy the company of animals. They work with other animal experts. They share their love of animals with others.

ZOO JOBS

Zoos also hire mechanics, computer programmers, architects, and librarians.

Zookeepers get to interact with the animals they love.

GLOSSARY

animal science
the study of animals that are under the control of humans

aquarium
a place where water animals and plants are kept for people to look at

behavior
the way in which a living being acts

biology
the study of life

degree
an academic award given to students after they complete a course of study

species
a group of plants or animals of the same kind that can produce offspring together

veterinarian
a doctor who takes care of animals

volunteer
someone who works without pay

OTHER JOBS TO CONSIDER

ANIMAL TRAINER

Many zoos and parks have animal shows. Animals perform tricks. Animal trainers train these animals. They make sure animals and people stay safe during the shows.

RESEARCHER

Researchers are scientists. They study wild animals at the zoo. They research specific questions about animal behavior.

ZOO EDUCATOR

Zoo educators know a lot about wild animals. They help zoo guests learn about the animals. They often focus on one or a few animals.

ACTIVITY

STUDY AN ANIMAL

Most large zoos have websites. Search online for a zoo near you. Explore the website. What animals are there? Which of the animals do you find most interesting? Choose one animal to study. Write down five questions about that animal. Try to find the answers online.

If possible, go to the zoo and visit that animal's exhibit. Many exhibits have information about the animals. What information can you find about the animal? If there is a zookeeper there, ask him or her your questions.

Share what you learned with family and friends. What are the most interesting facts about the animal? What might people want to know?

FURTHER RESOURCES

Thinking of a zookeeper career? Learn more here:

Career Kids: Zookeeper
https://careerkids.com/pages/zookeepers

Kidsville: Zookeeper
http://kidsvillenews.com/2015/04/kids/zookeeper/

Otfinoski, Steven. *Zookeeper*. New York: Cavendish Square, 2014.

St. Louis Zoo: So You Want to Be a Zookeeper?
www.stlzoo.org/animals/soyouwanttobeazookeeper

Curious about similar jobs? Check out this book:

Bedell, J. M. *So, You Want to Work with Animals? Discover Fantastic Ways to Work with Animals, from Veterinary Science to Aquatic Biology.* New York: Aladdin, 2017.

INDEX